"The Life of Journalists"

Sarwat Parvez

Maryland, USA. sarwatparvez@gmail.com

Contents

1. Introduction 3

2. Journalism Facing Odds in Pakistan 14

3. Journalists Facing Odds in India 31

4. Journalist's Problems Covering War Zone 45

5. Restricting Aljazeera News Channel by Israelis for Reporting 50

6. Restrictions on Media By the Israeli Government 54

7. Ukraine- Russian War Coverage 56

8. Biased USA Media 61

9. Critically Evaluate the Biased Media Coverage 62

10. Biased Coverage of Rohingya Muslims Suffering 69

11. Journalists Challenges Around the World 70

12. Raising Awareness about Journalists' Safety - 75

Introduction

The life of a journalist is marked by a relentless pursuit of truth, often under circumstances that test the limits of their courage and integrity. Journalists face many challenges from local reporters uncovering corruption in small towns to war correspondents reporting from the front lines. Political and governmental pressures are common, as authorities may attempt to sway or suppress information that doesn't align with their narrative. Journalists who stand firm against such pressures often find themselves at odds with powerful entities.

The risks escalate in regions where freedom of speech is not a given. Reporters may be harassed, detained, or even face life-threatening situations. The story of Anna Politkovskaya, a Russian journalist who reported on the Chechen wars and was subsequently murdered, is a stark reminder of the dangers faced by those who dare to report on conflict and corruption. Similarly, the assassination of Daphne Caruana Galizia, who investigated and exposed corruption in Malta, underscores the peril that comes with confronting criminal elements.

War correspondents carry the heavy burden of narrating the horrors of war while being in the crosshairs themselves. Marie Colvin, an American journalist who covered conflicts from the Balkans to the Middle East, tragically lost her life while reporting on the siege of Homs in Syria. Her legacy, however, continues to inspire journalists to bear witness to the truth, despite the dangers.

The life of a journalist is not just about-facing external threats; it also involves an internal struggle to maintain objectivity and fairness. The ethical dilemmas they encounter can be as taxing as the physical dangers. Deciding what to report and how to report it, while avoiding sensationalism and respecting the dignity of those affected, requires a delicate balance.

Despite the risks and challenges, many journalists are driven by a sense of duty to inform the public and hold those in power accountable. Their work is crucial for the functioning of a democratic society, as they shine a light on issues that would otherwise remain in the shadows. The life of a journalist is a testament to the resilience of the human spirit and the enduring quest for truth. It's a

career that isn't chosen lightly, but rather embraced with a full understanding of its weight and significance.

Journalists around the world continue to face significant threats and challenges that impede their ability to report freely and safely. Recent examples highlight the breadth and severity of these threats across different regions. In Afghanistan, journalists have fled the country due to the Taliban's takeover, which has led to a crackdown on media freedom and safety concerns for those reporting on the ground. Belarus has seen a similar exodus of journalists following the 2020 presidential election, with many facing arrests, violence, and censorship in the aftermath of widespread protests the regime.

In China, the situation remains dire for journalists who report on sensitive issues, such as human rights abuses or government corruption. Zhang Zhan, a citizen journalist who reported on the early stages of the COVID-19 outbreak in Wuhan, was sentenced to four years in prison for "picking quarrels and provoking trouble" after her critical reporting. Similarly, in Egypt, journalists like Mahmoud Hussein Gomaa face prolonged detention without trial, often in harsh conditions that pose serious health risks.

The situation is not limited to authoritarian states; even in democratic countries, journalists face legal threats, harassment, and violence. For instance, in India, journalists reporting on farmer protests have been charged with sedition, and in the United States, reporters covering racial justice protests have been arrested or injured by law enforcement while performing their duties. These instances demonstrate the global nature of the threats to press freedom and the importance of international support and legal protection for journalists.

The United Nations has recognized the plight of journalists in exile, many of whom continue to face threats from their home countries even while abroad. The international community has been called upon to provide better protection and support for these journalists, who play a crucial role in maintaining the flow of information and holding power to account. The courage and resilience of journalists worldwide serve as a reminder of the vital importance of press freedom and the need for constant vigilance to safeguard this fundamental right.

Zhang Zhan, a Chinese citizen journalist, became a symbol of the struggle for press freedom in the face of government censorship and repression. Her case garnered international attention after she was detained for her reporting on the early stages of the COVID-19 outbreak in Wuhan. Zhang was charged with "picking quarrels and provoking trouble," a broad and ambiguous charge frequently used against activists and dissenters in China. Despite the risks, Zhang bravely continued her work, providing a rare glimpse into the situation on the ground during the initial outbreak.

Her conviction led to a four-year prison sentence, which she served in its entirety, despite widespread calls from human rights organizations and foreign governments for her release. During her imprisonment, Zhang went on a hunger strike to protest her detention, which resulted in her hospitalization and further highlighted the harsh conditions faced by political prisoners in China. Her plight raised serious concerns about the treatment of journalists and the lengths to which authorities would go to suppress information deemed unfavorable.

Upon completion of her sentence, Zhang's release was expected, but it was shrouded in uncertainty as reports emerged of her disappearance. The United States Department of State expressed deep concern over her situation, emphasizing the arbitrary nature of her detention and the mistreatment she endured. Eventually, Zhang was confirmed to have been released, though the circumstances surrounding her freedom remained troubling. Her former lawyers and activists reported that she had limited freedom of movement and was under close surveillance by the police.

Zhang's case is a stark reminder of the perils faced by journalists in authoritarian regimes and the importance of international advocacy for press freedom. It underscores the need for vigilance in protecting the rights of those who dare to speak truth to power and the ongoing struggle for transparency and accountability. Zhang Zhan's courage and determination continue to inspire journalists and activists around the world, serving as a testament to the enduring spirit of those committed to uncovering the truth, no matter the cost.

In China, journalists face a myriad of challenges that stem from stringent state control over the media and the government's efforts to shape the narrative both domestically and internationally. Chris Buckley, a veteran journalist with the New York Times, had to leave China in 2020 after the government declined to renew his visa. His experience reflects a broader pattern of foreign journalists being expelled or facing visa renewals declined as part of a larger diplomatic tit-for-tat between China and the United States.

Bethany Allen-Ebrahimian, a journalist with Axios, has also faced significant hurdles in reporting on China. Despite her extensive experience covering China-related topics, she has never been able to secure a long-term journalist visa for the country, limiting her ability to report from within its borders. This has forced her, like many others, to cover China from outside, often relying on remote sources and second-hand information, which can affect the depth and immediacy of reporting.

The Foreign Correspondents' Club of China has highlighted the increasing difficulties for journalists in the country, including surveillance, harassment, and even tracking by drones. These intensified barriers to independent reporting pose significant risks to journalists and hinder their ability to provide accurate, on-the-ground coverage.

Journalists who are based in China, particularly in the south and coastal areas, often chafe at the restrictions imposed by Beijing. They are required to wait for the state-run Xinhua News Agency's version of events before reporting on certain stories, even urgent ones like natural disasters. This restriction not only delays the dissemination of information but also ensures that the government's perspective is the first to be heard.

The challenges faced by journalists in China are not limited to foreign correspondents. Domestic journalists also operate under heavy scrutiny and risk repercussions if they step out of line. The case of Gao Yu, an outspoken Chinese journalist who was detained on charges of leaking state secrets, exemplifies the dangers faced by local reporters. Despite international outcry, Gao was sentenced to seven years in prison, showcasing the severe penalties for those who defy the government's media controls.

These examples underscore the complex and often perilous landscape for journalism in China. The government's tight grip on the media, combined with the use of legal and extralegal measures to suppress dissenting voices, creates an environment where reporting the truth can be a risky endeavor. Despite these challenges, journalists both within and outside of China continue to find ways to shed light on critical issues, often at great personal cost. Their resilience and commitment to journalistic integrity serve as a beacon for press freedom and the right to information worldwide.

Recent stories reported by foreign journalists in China have highlighted a range of critical issues, despite the challenges and restrictions they face. One significant area of focus has been the treatment of the Uyghur population in Xinjiang, with reports uncovering the extent of the surveillance and re-education camps that have drawn international condemnation. Journalists have also reported on the tightening grip on Hong Kong's freedoms and the subsequent pro-democracy protests, providing insights into the evolving political landscape and the local and global implications.

The COVID-19 pandemic's origins and China's handling of the initial outbreak in Wuhan have been subjects of intense scrutiny, with foreign reporters uncovering details that contradicted official accounts, despite facing threats and obstruction in their reporting. Environmental issues have also been a focal point, with stories exposing the impact of China's rapid industrialization on pollution levels, biodiversity loss, and climate change, shedding light on the environmental cost of economic growth.

Economic stories have delved into the realities of China's economic policies, trade practices, and their global ramifications, including the Belt and Road Initiative and the country's role in international trade disputes. Additionally, the human rights situation, including the crackdown on dissent and the silencing of activists and lawyers, has been persistently covered, drawing attention to the ongoing struggle for civil liberties in the country.

These stories, often reported at great personal risk, underscore the vital role that foreign journalists play in bringing to light issues of global significance from within China's borders. Their work continues to inform international audiences and policy discussions, contributing to a more nuanced understanding of China's complex social, political, and economic dynamics. Despite the obstacles, these journalists' commitment to uncovering the truth remains unwavering, reflecting the enduring importance of press freedom and the pursuit of transparent and accountable reporting.

Journalism Facing Odds in Pakistan

Journalism in Pakistan operates within a complex and challenging environment, where the pursuit of press freedom is often met with resistance and significant risks. The constitution of Pakistan guarantees freedom of expression, yet journalists in the country frequently encounter obstacles that impede their ability to report freely and safely. Over recent years, the media landscape has been characterized by attacks from various fronts, including targeted assaults, legal pressures, and a pervasive narrative that undermines the credibility of journalists.

The Pakistan Press Foundation (PPF) has been instrumental in advocating for higher standards of journalism in Pakistan. It aims to promote and defend freedom of expression both domestically and internationally. The PPF's efforts include organizing training programs for journalists, conducting research, and documenting violations against the press. These initiatives are crucial for enhancing the professional skills of journalists and raising awareness about the social, political, and human rights issues that impact their work.

Despite these efforts, the challenges persist. The media has faced an increase in legislation that sets stringent guidelines on acceptable content, leading to cases being registered against journalists. Physical assaults, harassment, and online threats, particularly against women journalists, are not uncommon. The government's rhetoric has at times contributed to a climate that is hostile to free press.

The year 2020 presented unique challenges for Pakistani journalists, as they navigated the dual threats of COVID-19 and increased censorship. The pandemic claimed the lives of several media workers and infected many others, posing a significant health risk for those covering the crisis. Journalists had to balance the demands of reporting on the spread of the virus with the need to adhere to safety protocols, often putting themselves at risk in the process.

In addition to health concerns, journalists faced aggressive forms of censorship. Social media content became a particular target, with policies developed to regulate online expression and cases filed against media workers for their posts. The regulatory body overseeing broadcast media, the Pakistan Electronic Media Regulatory Authority

(PEMRA), was notably active, taking channels off the air and enforcing content restrictions.

The gendered nature of attacks on press freedom was also highlighted, with women journalists being subjected to specific threats and harassment. This underscores the need for a concerted effort to address the unique challenges faced by women in the field.

In response to these challenges, the Pakistani government has enacted legislation aimed at protecting journalists and media professionals. The Protection of Journalists and Media Professionals Act, 2021, is one such measure designed to ensure the independence, impartiality, safety, and freedom of expression of journalists. However, the effectiveness of this legislation in practice remains to be seen.

Efforts to improve the standard of journalism in Pakistan have also included the introduction of certification programs. These programs, developed in consultation with senior Pakistani journalists, aim to provide a holistic approach to media education, covering the basics of editing and reporting. Such initiatives are vital for the continued development of journalistic standards in the country.

In summary, while the standard of journalism in Pakistan faces numerous challenges, there are ongoing efforts to improve the situation. Organizations like the PPF and legislative measures are working towards a freer and fairer journalistic environment. However, the reality on the ground indicates that much work remains to be done to ensure that journalists can operate without fear of reprisal and with the full protection of their rights. The international community's role in supporting Pakistani journalists and advocating for press freedom is more important than ever, as these journalists continue to strive for truth and accountability in the face of adversity.

Journalists in Pakistan have been facing an increasingly hostile environment, with numerous reports of threats, assaults, and even abductions. One of the more prominent cases involved Asad Ali Toor, a journalist who was assaulted in his own home by unidentified assailants in May 2021. The attackers, who claimed to be from a security agency, interrogated Toor about his sources of funding and confiscated his electronic devices. This incident followed charges of sedition that had been filed against Toor in September 2020, which were later dismissed by a court.

Another alarming incident occurred in April 2020 when Absar Alam, a television journalist known for his critical stance against the government, was shot and wounded outside his residence in Islamabad. Before this, Alam had faced charges of sedition and high treason for his social media posts criticizing the government.

The case of Matiullah Jan is also notable; he was abducted in broad daylight in Islamabad in July 2020, just a day before he was due to appear before the Supreme Court. Although he was released after a few hours, the abduction was widely viewed as an attempt to intimidate him due to his outspoken reporting.

In August 2022, Ilyas Samoo, a journalist and president of the local Bandar Press Club, was arrested in Sindh province. It is believed that his arrest was in retaliation for his journalistic work, highlighting the ongoing risks faced by journalists in the region.

These incidents are part of a broader pattern of harassment and intimidation that journalists in Pakistan must navigate. The space for dissent and the provision of information of public importance is rapidly shrinking, with journalists and human rights defenders at particular risk of censorship, physical violence, and arbitrary detention. The frequency and audacity of these attacks underscore the perilous conditions under which journalists operate in Pakistan and the urgent need for effective measures to ensure their safety and freedom of expression.

Journalists in Pakistan continue to navigate a treacherous landscape marked by systemic censorship, violence, and constraints on free speech. The media environment is increasingly authoritarian, with journalists contending with a range of safety risks, including death threats, abduction, assault, violence, and intimidation. Between 2002 and 2022, 90 journalists were killed in the country, highlighting the extreme dangers of the profession in Pakistan.

The legal framework in Pakistan offers constitutional guarantees for freedom of speech and the press, but these are often undermined by "reasonable restrictions" imposed for reasons of national security, defense, or religion. These restrictions have been used to limit press freedom, particularly when reporting might offend decency, morality, or the official religion, Islam.

The recent case of Arshad Sharif, a 49-year-old TV journalist who was killed in Nairobi under mysterious circumstances, has raised serious concerns about the safety of journalists who report critically on the Pakistani government. Sharif had been living in exile after fleeing Pakistan to avoid detention on charges of sedition, and his family alleges government involvement in his murder.

In addition to physical threats, Pakistani journalists face a culture of fear and self-censorship, which limits coverage of critical issues such as human rights violations, corruption, and political repression. This self-censorship is particularly consequential during political and economic crises, where access to reliable information is essential.

The proposed Pakistani Media Development Authority (PMDA) and the "Removal and Blocking of Unlawful Online Content" regulation pose further threats to journalistic freedom. These measures could lead to arbitrary decisions without the possibility of appeal and give authorities the power to control and censor online content.

The situation is exacerbated by the treatment of minority communities, as evidenced by the kidnapping of Akash Ram, the marketing director at Bol Media Group, which has sparked concerns about the country's treatment of its Hindu community.

The International Day to End Impunity for Crimes against Journalists serves as a reminder of the urgent need for action to protect and promote the work of journalists and civil society activists in Pakistan. The international community's support is crucial in advocating for press freedom and the safety of journalists who play a vital role in maintaining the flow of information and holding power to account.

The challenges faced by media persons in Pakistan are not limited to external threats; they also include health problems, job cuts, salary cuts, layoffs, and the difficulty of accessing credible information. The compulsion to carry out COVID-19 reporting amidst the pandemic has added to the already significant challenges faced by journalists.

Despite these daunting conditions, journalists in Pakistan persevere in their efforts to report the truth and maintain the integrity of their profession. Their resilience in the face of adversity is a testament to the critical role that journalism plays in society, and the importance of continued vigilance in protecting the rights and safety of those who seek to inform the public. The standard of journalism in Pakistan, while facing numerous obstacles, is upheld by the courage and dedication of its media professionals. Their commitment to journalistic ethics and the pursuit of truth continues to shine a light on issues of public importance, even in the darkest of circumstances.

Journalists in Pakistan have faced a range of legal challenges that underscore the precarious nature of press freedom in the country. One notable case is that of Shahzeb Jilani, a journalist who worked for Dunya News and was charged with cyber terrorism, electronic fraud, and defamation in April 2019. The charges were based on his journalistic work, which included criticism of the military and judiciary. Although the case was later dismissed, it highlighted the use of the Pakistan Electronic Crimes Act (PECA) to target journalists.

Another significant case involved Bilal Farooqi, a news editor at The Express Tribune, who was arrested in September 2020 under PECA for his social media posts that were critical of the military and religious extremism. His arrest sparked widespread condemnation from journalist organizations and rights groups, who viewed it as an attempt to silence critical voices.

Similarly, Absar Alam, a senior journalist and former chairman of the Pakistan Electronic Media Regulatory Authority (PEMRA), faced legal challenges when he was shot and wounded by an unidentified assailant in Islamabad. Prior to the attack, Alam had been vocal about the military's influence over the media and had faced multiple legal notices and threats.

The case of Matiullah Jan, a seasoned journalist known for his critical reporting, is also noteworthy. He was abducted in broad daylight in Islamabad in July 2020, just hours before he was due to appear in the Supreme Court in a contempt case. Although he was released after several hours, the abduction was widely condemned as an act of intimidation against free speech.

These cases represent just a few examples of the legal challenges faced by journalists in Pakistan. They highlight the broader issue of the use of legal instruments, such as PECA, to suppress dissent and control the narrative. The situation for journalists in Pakistan remains fraught with danger, as they continue to navigate a landscape where legal threats are used as a tool to stifle freedom of expression and hold power to account. The resilience of these journalists, in the face of such adversity, is a testament to their commitment to upholding the principles of journalism and the public's right to know. Their struggles and the international support they receive are crucial in the ongoing fight for press freedom in Pakistan and around the world.

In Pakistan, journalists can adopt several strategies to defend themselves against legal threats, which are unfortunately a common challenge in the country. Firstly, staying well-informed about the laws that govern media and speech is crucial. Knowledge of the Pakistan Electronic Crimes Act (PECA), defamation laws, and other relevant legislation can help journalists understand their rights and the boundaries of legal reporting.

Building a strong network with fellow journalists, media organizations, and press freedom advocacy groups can provide a support system. These networks can offer solidarity, share best practices, and help when legal issues arise. Organizations like the Committee to Protect Journalists (CPJ) and Reporters Without Borders (RSF) often intervene on behalf of journalists facing legal challenges.

Seeking legal counsel from lawyers who specialize in media law is another important step. Legal professionals can offer guidance on how to navigate complex legal situations and may represent journalists in court if necessary. They can also help in filing petitions and advocating for the protection of fundamental rights.

Journalists should also document any threats or harassment they face and report these incidents to local and international watchdogs. This documentation can be used as evidence if legal action is taken against them and helps to raise awareness about the risks journalists face.

Adhering to the highest standards of journalism, including thorough fact-checking, maintaining objectivity, and avoiding sensationalism, can also serve as a defense.

Ethical reporting can protect journalists from accusations of libel or spreading misinformation.

In recent years, Pakistan has passed landmark laws aimed at improving the safety of journalists. Familiarizing themselves with these laws, such as the Protection of Journalists and Media Professionals Act and understanding how they can be applied for their defense is essential.

Finally, journalists can engage in advocacy to push for better legal protections and reforms that support press freedom. By voicing their concerns and working towards a more conducive environment for journalism, they can contribute to long-term changes that benefit the entire profession.

These measures, while not exhaustive, provide a framework for journalists in Pakistan to defend themselves against legal threats. It is a challenging landscape, but with the right knowledge, support, and resources, journalists can continue to report with a degree of security and confidence in their legal rights. The international community's role in supporting Pakistani journalists and advocating for press freedom is more important than ever, as these journalists continue to strive for truth and accountability in the face of adversity. The standard of journalism in Pakistan, while facing numerous obstacles, is upheld by the courage and dedication of its media professionals. Their commitment to journalistic ethics and the pursuit of truth continues to shine a light on issues of public importance, even in the darkest of circumstances.

Journalists in Pakistan have access to a variety of legal resources designed to support and protect their rights. One of the key resources is the Protection of Journalists and Media Professionals Act, 2021, which aims to ensure the independence, impartiality, safety, and freedom of expression of journalists and media professionals. This act provides a comprehensive framework for the protection of journalists, including the establishment of an Independent Commission for the Protection of Journalists and Media Professionals.

Another significant resource is the Pakistan Media Legal Review, produced by the Institute for Research, Advocacy and Development (IRADA). This annual review offers an in-depth analysis of legislative, legal, and judicial developments related to freedom of expression, the right to information, and digital rights in Pakistan. It serves as a valuable guide for journalists to understand the legal landscape and the challenges they may face.

The Pakistan Federal Union of Journalists (PFUJ) is a prominent organization that advocates for the rights of journalists. It provides legal assistance, supports journalists in cases of harassment or legal threats, and campaigns for better working conditions and press freedom. The PFUJ also works closely with international bodies to raise awareness about the issues faced by Pakistani journalists.

Legal Aid and Justice Authority Act, 2020, is another resource that establishes an authority to provide legal aid and ensure access to justice for vulnerable and marginalized groups, including journalists. This act can assist journalists who may not have the means to afford legal representation.

The Journalists Defense Committee (JDC) of the Pakistan Bar Council (PBC) is a dedicated body that offers legal support to journalists facing legal challenges. The JDC works to defend journalists in court and provides advice on legal matters.

In addition to these resources, there are various training programs and workshops available for journalists to enhance their understanding of media law and their rights. These programs are often organized by media advocacy groups and legal experts, aiming to equip journalists with the knowledge and skills needed to navigate the legal system effectively.

It's important for journalists in Pakistan to be aware of these resources and to utilize them when facing legal challenges. The support provided by these acts, organizations, and programs is crucial for the protection of press freedom and the safety of journalists in the country. The international community also plays a role in supporting these efforts, ensuring that Pakistani journalists have the necessary legal backing to carry out their essential work. The resilience and determination of journalists, bolstered by these legal resources, contribute to the ongoing struggle for a free and fair press in Pakistan. The Protection of Journalists and Media Professionals Act, 2021, and the efforts of organizations like IRADA and the PFUJ, are vital components in the defense of journalistic rights and the promotion of press freedom in the region.

Journalists Facing Odds in India

Journalism in India, much like in many parts of the world, is a profession that demands courage, resilience, and a steadfast commitment to the truth. Journalists in India navigate a complex landscape marked by diverse challenges that range from political pressures to personal safety risks. The country's vast media landscape is vibrant and competitive, yet it is not immune to the global trend of shrinking press freedoms. Political interference often manifests in subtle and overt forms, influencing the editorial policies of media houses and, at times, leading to censorship or self-censorship among journalists. The legal system, too, can be a double-edged sword; while it provides mechanisms for journalists to defend their work, it can also be used to intimidate and silence them through strategic lawsuits against public participation (SLAPPs) and other legal pressures.

The safety of journalists is a pressing concern, with reports of attacks and even fatalities among those who dare to report on sensitive issues. In recent years, India has witnessed a worrying trend of violence against journalists, with some paying the ultimate price for their dedication to uncovering the truth. The Committee to Protect Journalists has highlighted the dangers faced by

Indian journalists, noting that 2021 was one of the deadliest years for reporters in the nation. This violence is not just physical; online harassment, particularly against female journalists, has become rampant, creating an atmosphere of fear and intimidation.

Despite these challenges, Indian journalists continue to uphold the principles of democracy by informing the public and holding power to account. They report from conflict zones, investigate corruption, and provide critical analysis of government policies. Their work is essential for the functioning of a healthy democracy, ensuring transparency and fostering informed public discourse. The role of independent journalists is particularly noteworthy; without the backing of large media organizations, they rely on their tenacity and the support of their readership to bring important stories to light.

The international community, including organizations like Reporters Without Borders, closely monitors the situation of press freedom in India. The country's ranking on the World Press Freedom Index has been a point of concern, reflecting the need for continued vigilance and advocacy for the rights of journalists. The resilience of India's journalists, in the face of adversity, is a testament to their commitment to their profession and the critical role they play in safeguarding the pillars of democracy. Their stories are not just about the challenges they face but also about their unwavering spirit and the impact of their work on society. It is this spirit that continues to drive the narrative of journalism in India, inspiring the next generation of reporters to carry the torch of truth forward.

Recent incidents in India have underscored the perils that journalists face while performing their duties. For instance, there have been reports of an activist protesting against the arrest of a news website editor and its administrator after raids on journalists' homes in New Delhi, highlighting the threats and challenges journalists frequently encounter. In another case, Sébastien Farcis, a French journalist based in New Delhi, was compelled to leave the country, which has raised concerns about the pressures foreign journalists face and the implications for their families and livelihoods.

Moreover, the legal landscape for journalists in India remains fraught with challenges. Reporters Without Borders, along with national civil society organizations, has called upon the Indian government to adopt urgent measures to ensure the protection of journalists and the freedom of the press. These recommendations come in the wake of various instances where journalists have been targeted for their reporting.

The BBC has reported on the broader issue of journalists in India coming under attack, particularly in the context of covering sensitive topics like the farmers' protests. Journalists have faced charges including sedition and making statements detrimental to national integration, which has sparked significant concern among rights groups and fellow journalists.

Human Rights Watch has also highlighted the growing restrictions on media freedom in India, noting the arrest of journalists on spurious terrorism and sedition charges, and the targeting of critics and independent news organizations, including raids on their workplaces. This environment of intimidation and legal pressure significantly hampers the ability of journalists to report freely and critically.

These examples are indicative of the broader pattern of challenges faced by journalists in India, which include not only legal and political pressures but also threats to their personal safety and freedom of expression. The resilience of Indian journalists in such an environment is commendable, as they continue to strive for fair and independent journalism despite the risks involved. Their dedication to bringing forth the truth plays a crucial role in maintaining democratic processes and ensuring accountability. The international community's monitoring and advocacy are vital in supporting these journalists and promoting press freedom in India.

The media landscape in India is often criticized for its perceived bias towards the government, with allegations that many television channels and newspapers prioritize the government's narrative over impartial reporting. This phenomenon is not unique to India; media bias is a global issue where news outlets may align with political entities for various reasons, including financial incentives, ideological similarities, or regulatory pressures. In India, the relationship between the media and the government has come under scrutiny, particularly concerning how it affects the dissemination of information and the public's ability to receive a balanced view of events.

The Stimson Center has discussed the impact of widespread media bias on Indian democracy, emphasizing that the media should serve to inform rather than influence the public. It has been reported that the Indian government's allocation of advertising funds can significantly influence media outlets' operations and editorial policies. Outlets that align with government initiatives often receive more funding, which can lead to unbalanced reporting and a media landscape that favors the incumbent government.

Furthermore, the BBC has highlighted instances where journalists in India have faced legal challenges, including sedition charges, for reporting on sensitive issues such as the farmers' protests. These cases raise concerns about the freedom of the press and the ability of journalists to report without fear of reprisal. The World Press Freedom Index, compiled by Reporters Without Borders, has also reflected concerns about the state of press freedom in India, with the country's ranking being a point of concern for those advocating for journalistic independence.

The issue of media bias extends beyond just the relationship with the government. Professional laxity leading to inaccuracies and a class bias in the choice of news coverage are other significant barriers to quality journalism in India. These factors contribute to a media environment that may not always provide the most accurate or comprehensive portrayal of events.

In summary, while many Indian media outlets are accused of serving as the "butter of the government," it is essential to recognize the complex factors that contribute to this situation. Financial dependencies, legal pressures, and professional challenges all play a role in shaping the media's reporting. The need for independent journalism that can operate without undue influence remains a critical aspect of a healthy democracy, ensuring that the public has access to diverse perspectives and information. The resilience of journalists who continue to report with integrity, despite these challenges, is crucial for maintaining the democratic process and ensuring accountability in governance.

Discerning between biased and unbiased reporting is a critical skill in an era where information is abundant and comes from myriad sources. To navigate the media landscape effectively, consumers can employ several strategies. Firstly, consider the source of the information; reputable outlets commit to accuracy and accountability, often demonstrated through transparent correction policies and ethical standards. Secondly, analyze the language used in the reporting; biased reports may use sensationalist or emotionally charged words to sway the reader's opinion. Thirdly, look at the diversity of perspectives presented; a balanced report will include multiple viewpoints, especially from those directly affected by the issue.

It's also beneficial to check for the presence of supporting evidence. Reliable reports are typically backed by verifiable data and sources, whereas biased reporting may rely on uncorroborated claims or omit key facts. Additionally, understanding the ownership and funding of a media outlet can provide insights into potential biases, as owners may influence the editorial direction to align with their interests. Media literacy education, which is increasingly being incorporated into school curricula, can equip individuals with the tools to critically evaluate news content.

Furthermore, cross-referencing information across different outlets can highlight discrepancies and reveal biases. Tools like the AllSides Media Bias Chart offer a visual representation of where various news sources fall on the political spectrum, aiding in the identification of potential slant. Similarly, fact-checking websites can help verify the accuracy of reports and uncover any misleading statements.

In essence, discerning bias requires a combination of critical thinking, awareness of media dynamics, and proactive verification. By employing these methods, consumers can cultivate a more nuanced understanding of the news they consume and make informed decisions based on a comprehensive view of the information available. It's a skill that not only enhances one's media consumption experience but also contributes to a more informed and engaged society. The ability to distinguish between biased and unbiased reporting is not just beneficial; it's essential for the health of a democratic society where information is power. Engaging with a variety of news sources, questioning the information presented, and seeking out original sources where possible are all practices that can help achieve this goal.

The state of press freedom in India has been a subject of intense scrutiny and concern. Journalists like Ravish Kumar, who have been vocal and critical of the government, have faced significant challenges. Ravish Kumar, a prominent Indian journalist and former Senior Executive Editor of NDTV India, resigned from his position following the acquisition of NDTV by a business tycoon with close ties to the ruling party. This event raised alarms about the independence of the press in India, as Kumar was known for his critical and analytical reporting on the government's policies and actions.

The broader landscape for journalists in India is fraught with difficulties. Reports indicate a pattern of intimidation, threats, and violence against journalists, particularly those who are critical of the government or report on sensitive issues. The World Press Freedom Index has ranked India poorly, reflecting the challenges faced by the media in upholding free speech and expression within the country. Journalists have been charged with sedition and other serious offenses for their reporting, which has been seen as an attempt to stifle dissent and control the narrative.

The situation is exacerbated using social media to target journalists with harassment and threats, including death threats. This online trolling often translates into real-world violence, creating an environment of fear and self-censorship among journalists. The government's use of legal notices and internet shutdowns further impedes the ability of journalists to report freely and access information.

Recent incidents in India have highlighted the increasing challenges faced by journalists. In one notable case, several journalists were charged with sedition and other serious offenses after reporting on a farmers' protest, which turned violent in Delhi. The charges were based on their coverage of the event and the dissemination of the family's account of a protester's death, which contradicted the official police version.

Another alarming example involved the news website NewsClick, which came under investigation for allegedly receiving funds from China. Indian police conducted raids on the homes and offices of several of its journalists, which critics have described as an attack on one of India's few remaining independent news outlets. These raids followed similar actions against other media organizations, such as the BBC's New Delhi and Mumbai offices, which were searched over accusations of tax evasion.

The situation for journalists in India is further complicated by the prevalence of violence. For instance, NDTV's Mariyam Alvi and cameraperson Sushil Rathee were attacked by a mob in Northeast Delhi. Additionally, journalists from The Hindustan Times were threatened by a mob, asked to prove their religious identity, and chased.

Such incidents create an atmosphere of fear and intimidation, which can lead to self-censorship and hinder the free flow of information.

Moreover, there have been instances where journalists have been targeted through social media, with lists circulating online that identify them as "anti-Hindu" or as "Indian agents". This has led to police investigations and, in some cases, physical attacks on journalists while they were reporting. The pattern of violence and legal action against journalists in India raises serious concerns about the state of press freedom and democracy in the country. These cases underscore the need for greater protection for journalists and the upholding of free speech as a fundamental right.

In this climate, the role of journalists becomes even more crucial, as they strive to uphold the principles of democracy and inform the public. The challenges faced by journalists in India underscore the need for a robust and independent press, capable of holding power to account and safeguarding the democratic process. The international community and local institutions need to support journalists and advocate for the protection of press freedom in India. The courage and resilience of journalists like Ravish Kumar serve as a reminder of the importance of journalism in a democratic society.

To enhance the protection of journalists in India, a multifaceted approach is required, combining legal reforms, safety protocols, and support networks. Legal protections can be strengthened by reforming laws that are often misused to restrict press freedom, such as defamation and sedition laws, ensuring swift and fair legal processes in cases involving press freedom violations. Establishing an independent regulatory framework that can act as a buffer between the government and the media is also crucial.

Educational initiatives that inform journalists of their rights, legal remedies, and protection measures available under Indian law are essential. Resources like the "Know Your Rights Guide for Journalists in India" provide valuable information on how journalists can navigate legal challenges and what actions to take if their rights are infringed.

On-the-ground safety measures include providing journalists with safety training, especially those reporting from conflict zones or on sensitive issues. News organizations can implement emergency protocols and provide protective gear to reduce the risk of harm. Additionally, establishing a rapid response system for incidents of violence or threats can ensure that journalists receive immediate assistance and support.

Support networks play a pivotal role in protecting journalists. These networks can offer legal aid, counseling services, and create solidarity among media professionals. International organizations like the Committee to Protect Journalists (CPJ) and Reporters Without Borders (RSF) can collaborate with local institutions to monitor and advocate for journalists' safety.

Digital security is another critical area, as online harassment and cyber threats are prevalent. Training journalists in digital security practices, using encrypted communication tools, and raising awareness about cyber threats can help mitigate these risks.

Lastly, public awareness campaigns can highlight the importance of press freedom and the challenges faced by journalists. Such campaigns can foster public support for journalists and put pressure on authorities to act against those who threaten press freedom.

In summary, protecting journalists in India requires a comprehensive strategy that addresses legal, physical, and digital security challenges, while fostering a culture that values and upholds the freedom of the press.

Journalist's Problems Covering War Zone

To enhance the protection of journalists in India, a multifaceted approach is required, combining legal reforms, safety protocols, and support networks. Legal protections can be strengthened by reforming laws that are often misused to restrict press freedom, such as defamation and sedition laws, ensuring swift and fair legal processes in cases involving press freedom violations. Establishing an independent regulatory framework that can act as a buffer between the government and the media is also crucial.

Educational initiatives that inform journalists of their rights, legal remedies, and protection measures available under

Indian law are essential. Resources like the "Know Your Rights Guide for Journalists in India" provide valuable information on how journalists can navigate legal challenges and what actions to take if their rights are infringed.

On-the-ground safety measures include providing journalists with safety training, especially those reporting from conflict zones or on sensitive issues. News organizations can implement emergency protocols and provide protective gear to reduce the risk of harm. Additionally, establishing a rapid response system for incidents of violence or threats can ensure that journalists receive immediate assistance and support.

Support networks play a pivotal role in protecting journalists. These networks can offer legal aid, counseling services, and create solidarity among media professionals. International organizations like the Committee to Protect Journalists (CPJ) and Reporters Without Borders (RSF) can collaborate with local institutions to monitor and advocate for journalists' safety.

Digital security is another critical area, as online harassment and cyber threats are prevalent. Training journalists in digital security practices, using encrypted communication tools, and raising awareness about cyber threats can help mitigate these risks.

Lastly, public awareness campaigns can highlight the importance of press freedom and the challenges faced by journalists. Such campaigns can foster public support for journalists and put pressure on authorities to act against those who threaten press freedom.

In summary, protecting journalists in India requires a comprehensive strategy that addresses legal, physical, and digital security challenges, while fostering a culture that values and upholds the freedom of the press.

Journalists around the world face significant risks as they strive to report the truth and inform the public. The dangers they encounter can range from harassment and imprisonment to violence and even death. For example, UNESCO reported that between 2016 and the end of 2020, 400 journalists were killed, and the rate of impunity for these killings remains alarmingly high. Journalists covering protests have increasingly become targets of attacks by security forces and protestors alike. In 2020, UNESCO's survey revealed that 73% of women journalists experienced online violence, which sometimes led to offline attacks.

The COVID-19 pandemic has introduced new challenges for journalists, with increased harassment and a higher risk of contracting the virus. The Press Emblem Campaign reported that at least 1,967 journalists died after contracting COVID-19 between March 2020 and February 2022. In Mexico, a particularly harrowing example is the killing of three journalists within just three days, contributing to a total of 11 reporters killed since the beginning of the year. Chilean journalist Francisca Sandoval succumbed to injuries after being shot while covering a protest.

The rise in authoritarianism globally has made journalism more perilous. Leaders in various countries have vilified the press, contributing to a climate where violence against journalists is more likely to occur. The term "fake news" has been weaponized, leading to increased hostility towards the media and exacerbating the threats they face. Journalists are essential in maintaining the free flow of information, yet they are often treated as adversaries, especially when their reporting threatens to expose the actions of powerful entities.

The internet, while a tool for information dissemination, has also compounded these threats. Online harassment campaigns, disinformation, and increased surveillance have made the digital space a battleground for journalists. They face coordinated defamation campaigns, phishing attacks, and other forms of cyber violence aimed at silencing them. These threats not only affect their professional work but also their personal safety and mental well-being.

In conclusion, journalists across the globe continue to work under dangerous conditions, often putting their lives at risk to deliver news and uphold the principles of free speech and democracy. Their courage and dedication to their profession play a critical role in ensuring that societies remain informed and free. The international community, media organizations, and governments must work together to improve the safety of journalists and ensure that those who commit crimes against them are held accountable. Disclaimer: This information is based on reports available up to 2021 and recent web search results; the situation may have evolved since then.

Restricting Aljazeera News Channel by Israelis for Reporting

The ban of Al Jazeera by Israel is a complex issue rooted in the broader context of media freedom, national security, and political dynamics. The Israeli government's decision to shut down Al Jazeera's operations within its borders was officially justified on the grounds of national security concerns. According to reports, the Knesset, Israel's parliament, passed a law on April 1 that allowed the temporary closure of foreign media outlets deemed a threat to security. This law was subsequently invoked to ban Al Jazeera, leading to the closure of its offices and the cessation of its broadcasts in Israel.

The move to ban Al Jazeera has been met with criticism from various quarters, including press freedom organizations, which argue that it represents a significant infringement on the freedom of the press. Critics suggest that the ban may be part of a broader strategy to control the narrative around the Israel-Palestine conflict, particularly considering Al Jazeera's extensive coverage of the region and its often-critical stance towards Israeli policies. The ban's implications extend beyond the immediate impact on Al Jazeera's ability to operate in

Israel, as it also affects the outlet's access to the West Bank and Gaza, areas where the Israeli government exercises significant control over media access.

Political analysts have interpreted the ban as a populist move aimed at appeasing certain segments of the Israeli public and the government's far-right coalition partners. These partners have historically expressed hostility towards Al Jazeera, accusing it of biased reporting and sympathizing with Palestinian perspectives. The ban also coincides with heightened tensions and violence in the region, suggesting a possible link between the timing of the ban and the government's desire to manage public perception during periods of conflict.

Al Jazeera has vowed to challenge the ban through legal channels, asserting that the actions taken by the Israeli government are illegal and constitute an attack on journalistic freedom. The network has a history of facing obstacles in various countries due to its coverage, which often challenges the official narratives of governments in the Middle East and beyond.

In conclusion, the ban on Al Jazeera by Israel raises important questions about the balance between national security and press freedom. It highlights the precarious position of media outlets operating in politically sensitive environments and underscores the need for vigilance in protecting the rights of journalists to report without undue interference. As the situation evolves, the international community will be watching closely to see how the legal challenges to the ban unfold and what this means for the future of press freedom in the region.

The legislative action taken by Israel to ban Al Jazeera is part of a broader trend where media outlets face restrictions and bans, especially in regions of political sensitivity or conflict. The law passed by the Knesset, which allows for the temporary closure of foreign news networks deemed a threat to national security, could potentially be applied to other media outlets as well. While the specific instances of other media outlets facing similar bans in Israel are not detailed in the search results, the law's broad language suggests that any foreign network could be subject to similar treatment if it is perceived to be harming Israel's national security.

This move to control media presence and narrative within a country's borders is not unique to Israel. Globally, there have been instances where governments have taken steps to restrict or ban media outlets that they view as hostile or contrary to their national interests. Such actions often draw criticism from international press freedom organizations, which view them as violations of the freedom of the press and the public's right to access diverse sources of information.

In the context of Israel, the ban on Al Jazeera has been the most prominent case in recent times, drawing significant international attention due to the network's wide reach and influence. The ban reflects the government's stance on media that provide coverage that is critical of its policies or sympathetic to the Palestinian cause. It also highlights the challenges that media outlets face in maintaining their operations in the face of governmental pressures.

The implications of such bans are far-reaching. They not only affect the media outlet's ability to report and operate within the country but also impact the public's access to information. When a media outlet is banned, the diversity of perspectives and narratives available to the public is reduced, which can lead to a more one-sided understanding of complex issues like the Israel-Palestine conflict.

Moreover, the use of national security as a justification for media bans raises important questions about the balance between a state's security interests and the principles of free speech and press freedom. It is a delicate balance that requires careful consideration, as overly broad or arbitrary application of such laws can lead to the suppression of legitimate journalistic activities.

In conclusion, while the search results do not specify other media outlets that have faced similar bans in Israel, the existence of the law itself is indicative of the potential for such actions. It underscores the precarious position of the press in areas of conflict and the need for vigilance in upholding the rights of journalists and media organizations to operate freely and without undue interference.

Restrictions on Media By the Israeli Government

The landscape of media reporting in Israel is complex and multifaceted. It's important to understand that various regulations and practices can influence the reporting process. For instance, foreign news entities in Israel, such as CNN, are subject to rules set by the Israel Defense

Forces (IDF) censor, which can limit the scope of coverage on sensitive issues. This means that reports on certain topics must be reviewed by the IDF censor, and this can impact the timeliness and content of the news being reported. Additionally, internal policies of news organizations can also affect reporting. For example, CNN requires all content related to Israel and Palestine to be reviewed by its Jerusalem bureau before publication, which has led to concerns about the impartiality of coverage.

Journalists in the region face significant risks and challenges, including arrests, threats, and censorship, which can make reporting on conflicts like the Israel-Gaza war exceptionally difficult. The Committee to Protect Journalists has documented multiple incidents of journalists being targeted while carrying out their work in Israel and the Palestinian territories. These challenges highlight the high risks associated with reporting in conflict zones and underscore the importance of journalistic freedom and safety.

It's also noteworthy that while the written press and online content are generally unregulated fields in Israel, they are still subject to ad hoc regulations enshrined in the penal and civil codes, and courts commonly resort to publication bans. This indicates that while there is some level of freedom, there are still constraints that can affect how the media operates and reports on events.

Understanding the nuances of media regulation and the challenges faced by journalists is crucial for a well-informed perspective on the reporting from this region. It's clear that while there are mechanisms in place that may scrutinize and potentially influence media coverage, the situation is not black and white, and there are ongoing debates and discussions about media freedom, censorship, and the ethical responsibilities of reporting in such complex environments.

Ukraine- Russian War Coverage

Journalists covering the Ukraine-Russian war are confronted with a multitude of challenges that impact both their safety and the integrity of the news they deliver. The war zone presents inherent dangers, with reporters risking their lives to provide firsthand accounts of the conflict. Beyond physical threats, journalists face pressure from various authorities, leading to censorship and political interference. For instance, there have been reports of Ukrainian journalists being drafted for the war as a form of retribution for their reporting. Additionally, the martial law imposed in Ukraine can be used to justify the seizure or control of media assets, raising concerns about the potential abuse of power without proper oversight.

The emotional toll on journalists is also significant, as many are covering the violent events unfolding in their own country, adding a layer of personal distress to their professional duties. This emotional involvement can lead to a challenging balance between reporting objectively and managing personal biases and trauma. Moreover, securing essential protective gear like body armor has been a difficulty, leaving journalists vulnerable in high-risk situations.

In Russia, the situation for journalists is equally dire. A law against "spreading fake news" about the military can result in heavy prison sentences, effectively silencing independent reporting on the war. This has led to the closure or suspension of several independent media outlets, and those that continue to operate do so at great risk.

Furthermore, evidence suggests that journalists may be deliberately targeted by Russian troops, increasing the peril of reporting from the front lines. The Committee to Protect Journalists has noted instances of journalists being injured or killed while covering the conflict, highlighting the extreme risks involved in war reporting.

The cumulative effect of these challenges is a media landscape in which obtaining and disseminating truthful, unbiased information becomes increasingly difficult. Journalists must navigate not only the physical dangers of war but also the intricate web of political and emotional factors that influence their work. Despite these obstacles, many continue to report with courage and determination, understanding the critical role they play in informing the public and preserving the principles of a free press. Their resilience in the face of adversity underscores the importance of journalism in times of conflict and the need for continued support to protect their ability to report freely and safely.

The war in Ukraine has seen a surge in courageous and impactful journalism that has brought the realities of the conflict to the global stage. One notable example is the ten-episode documentary series "Ukraine'22: Diaries of the War," which provides a poignant look at the lives of average citizens and soldiers during the war. The series has garnered significant attention, accumulated 1.5 million views and won a documentary award. It has been praised for its ability to inspire and inform viewers about the Ukrainian struggle for statehood and independence.

Another example of significant reporting comes from the Stanford scholar and former war journalist Janine Zacharia, who has discussed the unique aspects of the media coverage of this war. She notes the extensive coverage due to the upending of the post-World War II order and the potential for escalation into a larger confrontation with NATO. Zacharia also highlights the relatively easy access journalists have had to Ukraine, which has allowed for a substantial number of reporters on the ground, providing an unprecedented level of live reporting through tweets and social media posts.

In addition to these, investigative journalists in Ukraine are taking on the dangerous task of reporting from the frontlines. Their work has been essential in uncovering the carnage and chaos of the war, often at great personal risk. The reporting has not only informed the public but has also served as a historical record of the events unfolding in real-time.

The impact of these reports cannot be overstated. They have brought the world's attention to the humanitarian crisis, the bravery of the Ukrainian people, and the complexities of modern warfare. These journalists' dedication to uncovering the truth and informing the public has been a testament to the power and necessity of free press in times of conflict. Their stories have helped shape international understanding and response to the war, proving that even in the darkest of times, journalism can shine a light on the truth. The commitment of these reporters to their craft, despite the dangers, serves as a reminder of the vital role that journalism plays in society. Their work is not just about reporting facts; it's about telling the stories that would otherwise go untold, giving a voice to the voiceless, and holding those in power accountable. The war in Ukraine has been a stark reminder of the importance of independent journalism and the need to protect and support those who pursue it in the face of adversity.

Biased USA Media

The perception of media bias in reporting on the Israel-Palestine conflict is a complex issue with deep historical roots. Media outlets are often criticized for their coverage, with accusations of bias coming from all sides. Some argue that there is a pro-Israel bias, where Israeli narratives and perspectives are given more weight and sympathy, while Palestinian viewpoints are underrepresented or portrayed negatively. Conversely, others claim there is an anti-Israel bias, suggesting that media coverage is overly critical of Israel and sympathetic to Palestinians.

These perceptions of bias can be influenced by various factors, including the political leanings of a media outlet's ownership, the target audience, and the individual journalists' perspectives. Additionally, the geopolitical alliances and foreign policy positions of the country where the media outlet is based can also play a significant role. For instance, the United States has a longstanding alliance with Israel, which some suggest may influence how American media outlets report on the conflict.

Academic research on media bias tends to show mixed results, with some studies finding evidence of pro-Israel bias and others indicating a more balanced or even pro-Palestinian slant. It's important to note that media bias is not always intentional; it can result from unconscious biases, the availability of sources, and the framing of stories based on what is deemed newsworthy.

The debate over media bias in the context of Israel and Palestine is part of a larger conversation about the role of media in society and the challenges of reporting on complex international issues. It highlights the importance of media literacy and the need for consumers to seek out multiple sources of information to gain a more comprehensive understanding of the issues at hand. Ultimately, the question of media bias is not easily answered, as it involves subjective interpretations of coverage and the intricate dynamics of media production and consumption.

Critically Evaluate the Biased Media Coverage

To critically evaluate media coverage, individuals can adopt a multi-faceted approach. Firstly, one should consider the source of the information, examining the media outlet's reputation, history, and potential biases. It's also beneficial to cross-reference news stories with multiple sources, especially those with differing perspectives, to gain a broader view.

Analyzing the language used in the coverage can reveal a lot; look for loaded or emotive words that may betray a bias. Understanding the context is crucial; background research on the topic at hand can provide insight into the larger narrative. Checking the author's credentials and other articles they've written can offer clues about their viewpoint and reliability.

It's also wise to scrutinize the evidence presented. Are there citations or links to primary sources? Are the facts hold up under further investigation? Be wary of coverage that relies heavily on anonymous sources or lacks corroboration.

Another key aspect is to be aware of what is not being said. Omission of certain facts or viewpoints can be as influential as what is included. Pay attention to the framing of the story – what is the focus, and what might be getting downplayed or ignored?

Media literacy education can be incredibly valuable, teaching individuals how to critically assess media messages and the various techniques used to influence audiences. Engaging in discussions with others about media coverage can also challenge one's perceptions and foster a more critical approach.

Finally, supporting independent and investigative journalism can contribute to a more diverse media landscape, providing a counterbalance to mainstream media narratives. By taking these steps, individuals can become more discerning consumers of media, better equipped to navigate the complex flow of information in today's world.

Fact-checking news stories is a critical skill in the digital age, where misinformation can spread rapidly. To fact-check effectively, start by considering the source of the news. Reliable sources typically have a track record of accuracy and editorial oversight. Look for information about the publisher's credentials and check if the outlet is recognized by reputable fact-checking organizations.

Next, examine the author's background and other articles they've written. This can provide insight into their expertise and potential biases. Pay attention to the date of the article as well; outdated stories can be misleading when presented as current events.

Scrutinize the evidence presented in the story. Are there links to primary sources or data that support the claims? If the article cites research, look up the study to see if it has been interpreted correctly. Be wary of sensational headlines that don't reflect the content of the article, as these can be a sign of clickbait or misinformation.

Check for logical fallacies in the argumentation. Does the story make unfounded leaps in reasoning or use emotional appeals instead of facts? Analyze the language used; loaded or emotive words can indicate a lack of objectivity.

Consider what might be missing from the story. Are there alternative perspectives or relevant facts that have been omitted? This can skew the portrayal of the issue.

Use fact-checking websites and tools to verify information. Many organizations specialize in debunking false claims and can be valuable resources for verification.

Lastly, maintain a healthy skepticism and don't take information at face value. By applying these strategies, you can become more adept at discerning the truth in news stories and contribute to an informed public discourse.

Verifying images and videos shared on social media is crucial in an era where digital content can be easily manipulated. To start, reverse image searches are powerful tools; services like Google Reverse Image Search and TinEye allow users to trace the origin of an image or check if it has appeared online before. For videos, checking metadata can provide insights into when and where the video was recorded. Tools like InVID can help analyze videos frame by frame to spot inconsistencies.

Another step is to examine the context in which the image or video is shared. Look for any accompanying text or hashtags that could indicate a bias or a specific narrative. It's also helpful to check the profile of the person sharing the content to assess their credibility and to see if they have a history of sharing reliable information.

Geolocation tools can verify if the image or video was indeed taken at the claimed location. Google Earth and Google Street View can be used to cross-reference landmarks and other geographical details present in the content. Additionally, observing the weather, shadows, and even the position of the sun can help determine the plausibility of the time and date claimed.

For images, pay attention to details like shadows and reflections, which can reveal signs of tampering. Photo forensic tools can analyze images for digital alterations not visible to the naked eye. Social media platforms themselves sometimes provide tools to report or flag suspicious content, which can then be reviewed by their verification teams.

Building a network of trusted sources and individuals with expertise in various fields can also aid in the verification process. Engaging with these networks can provide quick insights into the authenticity of a piece of content.

Lastly, it's important to trust one's instincts. If an image or video elicits a strong emotional response or seems too good to be true, it may warrant a closer look. By combining these methods and maintaining a healthy skepticism, individuals can more effectively discern the authenticity of images and videos on social media. Remember, in the digital age, seeing should not always be believing. Always verify before trusting or sharing.

Identifying manipulated images involves a keen eye for detail and an understanding of digital editing techniques. Common signs include inconsistencies in lighting and shadows, which can betray an image's altered state. For instance, if the light source reflected in subjects' eyes doesn't match the surrounding lighting, or if shadows cast by objects seem to defy the light source, these can be indicators of manipulation. Warped or distorted backgrounds, often a result of editing tools, can also signal alterations.

Edges and borders are another area to scrutinize; they may appear unnaturally smooth or jagged, suggesting that a subject has been inserted or removed. Pixelation around specific features, changes in resolution, or color balance inconsistencies are telltale signs of tampering. Look for anomalies in reflections, especially in shiny surfaces where manipulated elements might lack the appropriate reflective properties.

Perspective errors can also reveal manipulations; objects added to a scene may not align with the photographic perspective, making them stand out. Text within images can provide clues as well; reversed or inconsistent text suggests digital alteration. Additionally, the presence of unnatural anatomical features, such as distorted hands or ears, can indicate AI-generated or edited content.

It's important to approach image verification with a critical mindset, using available tools and techniques to assess the authenticity of digital media. By being aware of these common signs, one can become more adept at discerning the real from the manipulated in the vast sea of digital imagery.

Biased Coverage of Rohingya Muslims Suffering

The international community has raised significant concerns about the treatment of the Rohingya people in Myanmar. There have been numerous reports of human rights violations and atrocities committed against them.

Various international bodies and human rights organizations are actively working to investigate these reports and bring attention to the plight of the Rohingya, advocating for their protection and holding those responsible accountable for their actions. It is crucial for the world to remain informed and engaged on this matter to ensure that justice is served, and human rights are upheld.

Journalists Challenges Around the World

Journalists around the world face a myriad of challenges that threaten not only their personal safety but also the very essence of press freedom. The profession, heralded as the cornerstone of democracy, is under siege as reporters encounter harassment, imprisonment, violence, and even death for fulfilling their duty to inform the public. The situation is particularly dire in regions where authoritarian regimes suppress free speech, and where corruption and crime make truthful reporting a hazardous task. UNESCO's report highlights a grim reality: journalism remains a deadly profession, with a staggering rate of impunity for crimes against journalists.

The digital landscape has further complicated matters, with online harassment and cyberattacks becoming commonplace. Women journalists face disproportionate levels of online violence, leading to self-censorship and psychological distress. The COVID-19 pandemic has exacerbated these issues, as journalists reporting on the crisis have faced increased risks, including a higher likelihood of contracting the virus. According to the Press Emblem Campaign, a significant number of journalists have lost their lives to COVID-19 contracted during their reporting duties.

Financial constraints pose another significant hurdle, with newsroom cutbacks leading to a lack of resources that hampers in-depth investigative journalism. The rapid evolution of social media and technology has transformed the media landscape, blurring the lines between fact and opinion and making it challenging for journalists to maintain credibility in the fight against misinformation. The Cision 2022 Global State of the Media report underscores the struggle journalists face in preserving their status as trusted news sources amid the proliferation of fake news.

Furthermore, journalists are increasingly targeted while covering protests, with attacks coming from security forces and protestors alike. This hostile environment is a testament to the growing dangers journalists face in their line of work. The challenges are not just external; ethical dilemmas, information overload, and the need for continuous learning and adaptation add to the complexity of the profession.

Considering these challenges, it is imperative for global efforts to focus on protecting journalists and upholding press freedom. The international community must rally to support those who brave the frontlines to deliver news, often at great personal cost. As guardians of information, journalists play a pivotal role in shaping an informed society, and their protection is essential for the health of democracies worldwide. Ensuring their safety and freedom is not just a matter of justice for the individuals affected but a fundamental requirement for the preservation of a free and fair society.

Recent cases of journalists facing danger are a stark reminder of the perils that come with the pursuit of truth and transparency. In the United States, the year 2021 saw a troubling number of press-freedom violations, including over 140 physical attacks on journalists, many of which occurred during protests. The US Press Freedom Tracker documented these assaults, highlighting the ongoing risks to journalists even in countries with established free press traditions.

Internationally, the UN Secretary-General has voiced concerns over the threats to journalists, noting that more than 70 journalists were killed in just one year, with most of these crimes remaining unsolved. The record number of journalists incarcerated, and the growing threats of violence and death underscore the gravity of the situation.

In Mexico, one of the most dangerous places for journalists, 18 were murdered in a single year, according to UNESCO. The climate of fear and violence has led to self-censorship and a decline in the quality of journalism, as survival becomes the primary concern for media workers.

Environmental journalists are not exempt from danger; a UNESCO report revealed that at least 749 journalists covering environmental issues faced attacks, including murder, violence, and legal harassment, between 2009 and 2023.

The digital realm presents its own set of challenges, with journalists regularly encountering online harassment, defamation campaigns, and cyberattacks. The use of "troll armies" to intimidate and discredit journalists critical of state institutions is a concerning trend that threatens press freedom.

Specific cases highlighted by TIME include Maria Ressa and Rappler in the Philippines, who face arrest and legal threats; and the detention of Reuters reporters Wa Lone and Kyaw Soe Oo in Myanmar under the Official Secrets Act.

These instances represent only a fraction of the dangers journalists face globally. The threats are multifaceted, ranging from physical violence to legal intimidation, and from online abuse to the psychological impact of constant danger. The protection of journalists and the safeguarding of press freedom remain critical challenges that require concerted efforts from governments, international organizations, and civil society to address. Ensuring that journalists can operate without fear is essential for the maintenance of a free and informed society.

Raising Awareness about Journalists' Safety

Raising awareness about journalist safety is a multifaceted endeavor that requires collective action from various sectors of society. Here are some strategies that can be employed:

1. Education and Training: Organizations like Reporters Without Borders offer safety guides for journalists, providing valuable information on how to stay safe in different reporting environments. Educational institutions can incorporate these resources into journalism curricula to prepare future journalists.

2. Public Campaigns: The Office of the United Nations High Commissioner for Human Rights (OHCHR) engages in raising awareness through public statements and events like World Press Freedom Day and the International Day to End Impunity for Crimes against Journalists.

3. Government Action Plans: Some governments have developed national action plans to enhance the safety of

journalists. For example, the UK government's plan includes free e-learning courses on journalism safety and resilience.

4. Support from Newsrooms: Newsrooms can develop policies to keep journalists safe online and provide support for those facing harassment. The Nieman Foundation offers guidelines for newsrooms to handle online harassment and secure social accounts.

5. Advocacy and Legal Support: Human rights organizations can monitor compliance with international standards and assist countries lacking infrastructure to protect journalists. They can also advocate for targeted sanctions against entities that threaten press freedom.

6. Utilizing Technology: Digital safety tools and training can help journalists protect their data and communications from surveillance and hacking attempts.

7. Solidarity Networks: Journalists can form networks to support each other, share safety protocols, and alert international bodies in case of emergencies.

8. Research and Reporting: Continuous monitoring and reporting on violations against journalists can help keep the issue in the public eye.

9. Engaging Policymakers: Lobbying for laws that protect journalists and ensure accountability for crimes against them is crucial.

10. Celebrating Courage: Recognizing and honoring journalists who risk their lives can inspire others and draw attention to the cause.

By employing a combination of these strategies, society can work towards creating a safer environment for journalists to perform their essential role in maintaining an informed public and a healthy democracy.

Success stories of journalist safety initiatives offer a beacon of hope in the challenging landscape of media work. One such example is the Securing Access to Free Expression (SAFE) initiative by IREX, which has been instrumental in supporting over 8,000 media professionals across 18 countries. SAFE's comprehensive approach includes hosting training and workshops, providing psychosocial support, and helping journalists anonymize their online presence. This initiative has been particularly effective, with 90% of participants who faced safety challenges after the training reporting that the knowledge and skills they acquired were very helpful in addressing these situations.

Another success story is the UN Plan of Action on the Safety of Journalists and the Issue of Impunity, which has spurred the creation of numerous projects aimed at promoting journalist safety in over 45 countries since 2009. This plan has been a cornerstone in the global effort to protect journalists and combat impunity for crimes against them.

The SAFE initiative's adaptability is also noteworthy. During the COVID-19 pandemic, it incorporated mitigation techniques and protocols into its training materials, offering remote training and publishing a risk assessment to support journalists' efforts to continue their work safely. This adaptability ensured that journalists could navigate the additional risks posed by the pandemic while keeping the public informed.

Furthermore, SAFE's focus on election-related violence and climate change has equipped journalists with the necessary knowledge and approaches to navigate these specific challenges. By creating materials on election-related violence and promoting awareness of risks faced by environmental-focused journalists, SAFE has addressed the evolving dangers in these areas.

The success of these initiatives is not limited to training and support. They also foster communities that advocate for and support independent journalism, creating a network of solidarity that can be crucial in times of crisis. The impact of these initiatives is evident in the increased awareness and preparedness among journalists, which ultimately contributes to a more informed and engaged public.

In conclusion, the success stories of journalist safety initiatives like SAFE and the UN Plan of Action reflect the positive outcomes that can be achieved through dedicated efforts to protect media workers. These initiatives serve as models for future programs and highlight the importance of continued support for the safety and freedom of journalists worldwide. The collective action and commitment demonstrated by these initiatives are essential for ensuring that journalists can continue to fulfill their vital role in society without fear for their safety.

Sarwat Parvez

Maryland, USA.

sarwatparvez@gmail.com